TOP 10

NATURAL PLACES TO VISIT IN HANOVER, NEW HAMPSHIRE

A WALKING GUIDE

By Steve Smith

1st edition
ISBN: 978-0-615-97216-9
Printed in China

On the cover: An October picnic on Huntington Hill

Back cover photo: The view of Mount Ascutney from Balch Hill

"Here nature calls from every direction."

— J.W. Goldthwaite, a Dartmouth professor,
writing about Hanover in 1913

ABOUT THIS GUIDE

At the very least, this book is meant to serve as a visual and physical reminder of the natural beauty in this historic area of New England. Ideally, this guide will also make it easy for everyone—adults, families with children, students—to quickly find a spot outside to take a walk, have a picnic, or to simply unwind in nature.

The book is presented in two ways. First, the descriptions provide the reader with an overall impression of the ten properties, and in some cases offer historical facts that may be of interest. The map page follows this theme, and lists the distance of each property from the Hanover Inn—chosen for its visibility—as well as the area's total acreage. Second, the "Suggested Walk" section offers a recommended walking trail, most of which are about a mile and a half long. However, these trails only touch on one way to experience these thousands of acres. In some cases, readers may just want to show up, and explore!

For many of the walks, using a mobile phone GPS app (Motion X-GPS is one example) is necessary to follow the trail descriptions. The GPS mobile phone apps are simple to use and work like a mileage tracker in a car. For GPS users, the Hanover Inn's address is 2 East Wheelock Street.

Every site in this book can be visited during all four seasons. Indeed, some, such as Huntington Hill, with its snowshoeing trails, and Oak Hill, with its cross-country skiing trails, are especially accessible in the winter. Mountain biking is allowed on Oak Hill and Storrs Pond.

As is true in most of New England, spring, late summer, and fall can be especially pleasant times to visit the land. Bugs can be bothersome in mid-summer. Hikers are discouraged from using trails during "mud season"—sometime between mid-March and April—when the ground is thawing and malleable.

Take a camera—you never know what you'll see. Without exception, all photos in this book, including those of wildlife, were taken at the actual sites.

INTRODUCTION

Known among the Abenaki as Cohos, or "white pine place," the Upper Connecticut River Valley has long been seen as a land of plenty. In 1752, the secretary of New Hampshire declared the region "the cream of the country," and in the following decade, Eleazar Wheelock chose Hanover over many other locations in the Northeast for the setting of Dartmouth College.

For more than 250 years, the town of Hanover has drawn adventurous, nature-loving spirits, among them the poet Robert Frost, the outdoorsman John Ledyard, and the writer Norman Maclean. Today, hikers, canoeists, photographers, writers, students, teachers, and many others continue to celebrate the land. There are towering white pines, cold streams with native brook trout, miles of packed-dirt walking trails, and rolling fields that seem landscaped for picnics. The Connecticut River runs alongside the town, the legendary Appalachian Trail cuts through it, and beckoning mountains are almost always in sight.

The land remains pristine thanks to the tireless work of many dedicated individuals and organizations, including the Hanover Conservancy, Dartmouth College, the Hanover Improvement Society, the town of Hanover, the Pine Park Association, and the student-run Dartmouth Outing Club. Please support their efforts.

1

Balch Hill

The Maple Trail wends along
the northeast side of Balch Hill.

The summit of Balch Hill offers striking views.

The only unforested summit in Hanover, Balch Hill provides sweeping views of the hills of Vermont, including distant Ascutney Mountain. A single, shapely maple tree stands in the middle of the grassy top. Nearby, tucked away in the woods, are the decaying trunks of massive, centuries-old oak trees. It's a picturesque setting, with stone walls, granite benches, birdhouses, and apple and crabapple trees. In late summer, the hill's monarch caterpillars can be found among the milkweed, and barred owls can often be heard in the evenings. Kite flying is a popular activity on the summit.

Monarch caterpillars feed on the milkweed on the summit.

The summit was protected in the 1970s by the Hanover Conservancy, the oldest local land trust in New Hampshire. The organization conducts ecological research on the hill, including measuring the impact of browsing deer on native vegetation.

Balch Hill Loop

DISTANCE: .92 MILES

The lovely summit of Balch Hill is only .26 miles away from the trailhead on this walk. Start at the large sign with a map across from the parking area on Grasse Road.

Walk .15 miles up the hill, arrive at an intersection, and take a left. Continue straight up hill (pass Link Trail on the left) and arrive at the summit. Circumvent the summit and find many spots ideal for a rest or picnic. Consider exploring the Hemlock, Hunter, and Piane trails that connect to the summit. (Pause GPS and restart at the summit.) When ready to depart, find the Fire Trail east of the large sign. Walk .34 miles and take a right onto the Maple Trail. Pass an old fire pond on the left. Take a right onto Garipay Trail at .45 miles, then take a right onto Hunter East Trail at .55 miles. Rejoin Grasse Road Trail at .76 miles, and take a left to return to the parking area.

The lone maple tree on the summit.

This bedded Whitetail Deer was seen along Hunter East Trail.

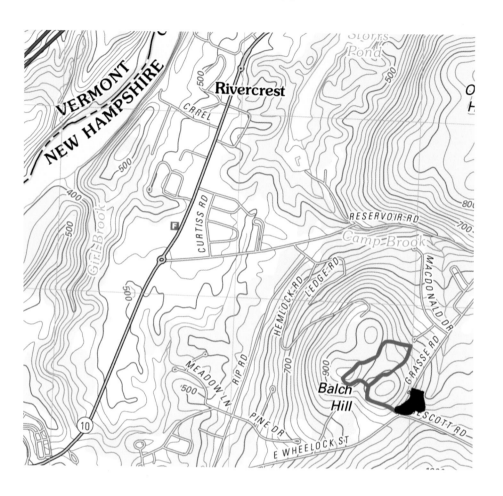

BALCH HILL AREA INFORMATION

43° 42' 38" N
72° 15' 26" W

Total acres: 85

Miles from Hanover Inn: 1.6

Driving directions/parking: Drive east on East Wheelock Street 1.6 miles and find parking area on left at the intersection of East Wheelock and Grasse Road.

2

Pine Park

The trail in the western section of Pine Park is level and shady.

Despite sitting on 90 acres, Pine Park remains a hidden gem nestled between the Dartmouth golf course and the Connecticut River. Beautiful examples of one of the nation's greatest trees, the Eastern White Pine, can be found in the park. From the mid-1600s to 1774, thousands of white pines—the property of the king of England—were shipped to Great Britain, as their light yet strong wood was perfectly suited for the Royal Navy's ship masts. As the trees grew scarce, prime specimens were marked with an arrow for the king. In his wonderful 1948 book, *A Natural History of North American Trees*, Donald Culross Peattie wrote that the arrow "infuriated the pioneer," and the king claiming the white pine was "one of the chief economic and psychological factors in the gathering storm of the American Revolution." Peattie also noted that, before the stars and stripes, the first emblem on the Revolutionary flag was a white pine.

This is a northwesterly view in Pine Park, looking across the Connecticut River towards Vermont.

This American Toad was found near a log off the trail.

As a walk through Pine Park demonstrates, the soil and air of Hanover are perfect for growing healthy white pines. Indeed, Peattie notes in his book that a whopping 240-foot-tall specimen was found in Hanover in the late 1700s. This is about 100 feet taller than the tallest white pines in New Hampshire today. "This would surpass anything in the eastern United States and would do credit to the Douglas fir of the West, and even the redwood," he wrote.

SUGGESTED WALK

Pine Park Loop

DISTANCE: 1.19 MILES

Sights on this leisurely walk include large pine trees, ferns, moss-covered logs, thrushes, and tree falls.

From the parking area, face the golf course and look west (left) and see a gravel golf cart path adjacent to a fence that appears to lead into the woods. This is the trailhead. To get there, leave the parking area and continue walking down the road 40 to 50 steps, so Occom Pond is to your left. Take a right onto 30-48 Occom Ridge Drive and almost immediately step onto the gravel golf cart path. After looking out for active golfers, walk down the gravel path and bear left, following the fence.

See the Pine Park sign and enter the trail straight into the woods.

Begin tracking hike at trail sign. Walk downhill, passing a building on your left at .13 miles. At the fork at .19 miles, bear left and follow the Connecticut River. At .47 miles, you'll see a large moss-covered log on your right in a clearing—this is a good picnic spot. At .56 miles, bear right. (Straight brings you to a second potential picnic area, next to the river.) At a four-way intersection at .61 miles, take a hard right onto the level trail and follow this back to its intersection with the original trail at .98 miles.

Thrushes are frequently heard, and sometimes seen, in Pine Park.

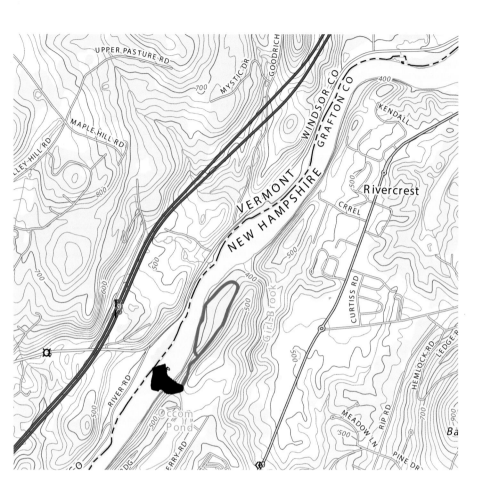

PINE PARK AREA INFORMATION

43° 42' 52" N

72° 17' 10" W

Total acres: 90

Miles from Hanover Inn: 1

Driving directions/parking: Drive north on College Street and take a left onto Maynard Street at .3 miles. Take a right at intersection with Rope Ferry Road. At .8 miles, reach the Dartmouth golf course and bear left. At .9 miles, just past the Hanover Country Club, see to your right a gravel parking area facing the golf course.

3

The Connecticut River

The view of Mink Brook, just prior to its confluence with the Connecticut River.

Located behind one of Hanover's oldest residential neighborhoods, the trails in this area provide a prime way to explore the Connecticut River. With its headwaters in a beaver pond near the Canadian border, the Connecticut is New England's largest river, flowing 410 miles south through four states to the Atlantic Ocean. The outlet into the Atlantic is 200 miles south from the Ledyard Bridge. Depending on your timing, as you stroll along the river you may see kayakers and canoeists, a bald eagle, or the Green Mountain Flyer rumbling along the train tracks on the Vermont side.

One of the early transportation highways of New England, the Connecticut River has been referenced so much in writing that it served as the subject of W.D. Wetherell's 311-page, 2002 anthology, *This American River: Five Centuries of Writing About the Connecticut*. Included in the book is Edwin M. Bacon's 1906 description of the river, in which he writes: "The predominating beauty of the River is sweet and winsome, rather than proud and majestic. It has its grand moods, but these are brilliant flashes which serve to enhance the exquisiteness of its gentler mien."

The view from a small cape in the Connecticut River.

SUGGESTED HIKE

River and Town Loop

DISTANCE: 1.9 MILES (NON-PAVEMENT, 1.31 MILES)

Get up close to the Connecticut River on this easy stroll that includes Hanover's Main Street. If you choose, end your hike with a stop for beverages and food at Molly's or another Hanover restaurant.

Start at the gate at the parking area and follow the brook on left. Arrive at a bench on the right at .53 miles. At .57 miles, take a left into the woods, and enjoy views of the river at .66 miles. (If you wish, take a left to see the confluence of the Mink and Connecticut.) Take a right and continue straight along the river, which bends left at .88 miles and leads at .92 miles to a spit of land with views of the Connecticut. This is a great spot for a picnic. Continue walking north along the river, then ascend the hill at .99 miles. Arrive at Maple Street at 1.06 miles and continue straight. Arrive at the intersection with Main Street at 1.48 miles. Take a left for restaurants and a right to return to the parking area.

This Karner Blue Butterfly (the state butterfly of New Hampshire) was seen off of the trail.

The habitat in this location supports dragonflies such as the Common Whitetail.

This American Redstart was seen near the entrance to the trail off of Route 10.

CT RIVER MINK BROOK AREA INFORMATION
43° 41' 41" N
72° 17' 25" W
Total acres: 15
Miles from Hanover Inn: .5
Driving directions/parking: Drive .5 miles south on
South Main Street, and park at the gravel lot, on the right,
just before the bridge leading over Mink Brook to the
town of Lebanon.

4

Storrs Pond

In the early morning the glassy surface of Storrs Pond mirrors the surrounding trees.

Storrs Pond was created in 1935.

Friendly people, cool and clear water, plenty of picnic tables, and a network of trails are what you'll find at Storrs Pond, a manmade body of water built in 1935 by the Hanover Improvement Society. The well-maintained area is open (for a fee) to swimming, canoeing, and fishing in the warmer months. Campers at Storrs Pond appreciate the spacious campsites, all of which are within walking distance to the pond. Families come from all over the Northeast to camp at Storrs Pond, and some choose it as their annual summer vacation destination. While the beach can be busy, you can easily find solitude by taking a few steps down a trail that circles the pond. The pond is located in a hollow surrounded by shade-giving pine trees. Because of this, it always seems to be cool at Storrs Pond, no matter how hot the day.

Black Bass are present, but hard to catch, in Storrs Pond.

SUGGESTED HIKE

Storrs Pond Loop

DISTANCE: 1.55 MILES

This walk offers up-close views of the lesser-explored, scenic sections of Storrs Pond.

Start at the two gateposts near Byrne Pavilion. Walk directly up the hill and bear right. At .13 miles, find a pleasant picnic area on the pine-needle-covered ground and a small swimming hole. At .32 miles, see the ropes course structure on your right. Continue straight on wide path and at the top of a hill, at .42 miles, take a left. Continue down the hill and at .48 miles pass the spur to the Rinker-Steele Natural Area. Arrive at the Storrs Pond dam at .57 miles. Continue up the hill (passing the sign for the Boy Scout area at .63 miles), then arrive at a field at .81 miles. Take a left. At an intersection at .91 miles, go straight and cut through the field to the pavilion. Pass the restrooms on your right and continue up the paved road, taking a left at the intersection with the gravel road at 1.18 miles. Stay on the road, arrive at the beach at 1.41 miles, and take a well-deserved dip in the pond. To return to vehicle, cross the bridge toward the restrooms and take a left on the dirt road through the campground.

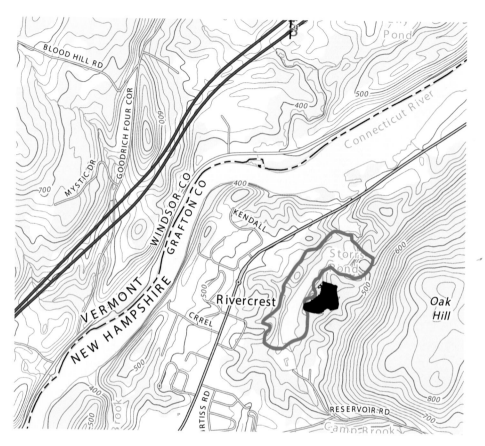

STORRS POND AREA INFORMATION

43° 43' 33" N

72° 15' 47" W

Approximate total acres: 15

Miles from Hanover Inn: 2.5

Driving directions/parking: Travel north on Route 10 and take right on Reservoir Road at 1.4 miles. Take a left to enter Storrs Pond at 2.12 miles. At 2.34 miles, arrive at the ticket booth. Almost immediately take a sharp right, before crossing the stream, onto the dirt road, and arrive at the Byrne Pavilion at 2.64 miles.

Note: In the off-season, the gate at the ticket booth will be closed, so you will park at the lot to the right and walk the .28 miles to the Byrne Pavilion.

5

Appalachian Trail
Velvet Rocks

Many moss-covered rocks that give the area its name are scattered around the Velvet Rocks area.

The Velvet Rocks Shelter is maintained by the Dartmouth Outing Club.

Stepping onto the Appalachian Trail (AT) is taking a step onto the pedestrian version of Route 95, the highway connecting the eastern United States. On the AT, you're as likely to encounter a Hanover resident as you are someone from hundreds of miles away with no knowledge of the town at all. Named for its moss-covered boulders, the Velvet Rocks section of the trail is maintained by the Dartmouth Outing Club.

In his book *A Walk in the Woods*, Bill Bryson (a onetime Hanover resident) referenced the AT in this memorable manner: "It seemed such an extraordinary notion—that I could set off from home and walk 1,800 miles through woods to Georgia, or turn the other way and clamber over the rough and stony White Mountains to the fabled prow of Mount Katahdin, floating in forest 450 miles to the north in a wilderness few have seen. A little voice in my head said: 'Sounds neat! Let's do it!' "

SUGGESTED HIKE

Velvet Rocks Shelter

DISTANCE: 1.64 MILES

This walk past an Appalachian Trail shelter ends at the Dartmouth athletic fields and the Hanover Co-op Food Store, a perfect spot to enjoy a celebratory trail-ending treat.

This Pileated Woodpecker was spotted on a foggy morning in the Velvet Rocks woods.

Start at the "Salt Reduction Zone" sign across from the parking area on East Wheelock Street. (The trail is a bit hidden.) Follow blue markers over rocks and past ferns and arrive at a dirt road at .17 miles. Take a right down the road and take a left back onto the trail at .21 miles. At .38 miles, see a sign marking the Ledyard Spring. Continue straight, following blue markers, and enter a small canyon with rock cliffs to your right. At the signpost at .52 miles, take a right onto the marked trail, over the rock cliffs. At .59 miles, arrive at another signpost, noting that Trescott Road (another name for East Wheelock) is .6 miles away. Take a left up the hill and enjoy a lookout with views to the southwest and a picnic spot at .67 miles. Continue down the trail to Velvet Rocks Shelter at .78 miles, then continue on to meet the Appalachian Trail at .97 miles, where you follow the white blazes down the hill and back into town. There are steep rocks at 1.46 miles.

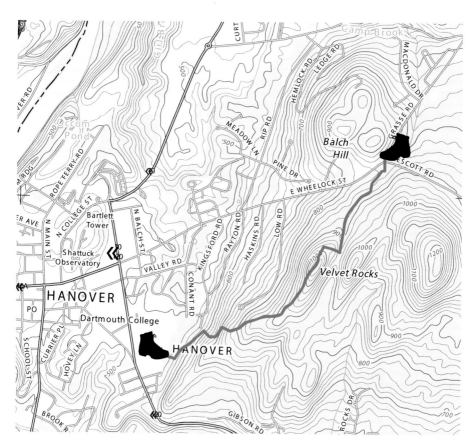

 VELVET ROCKS AREA INFORMATION

43° 42' 38" N

72° 15' 26" W

Total acres: 1,422

Miles from Hanover Inn: 1.6

Driving directions/parking: Drive east on East Wheelock Street
1.6 miles and find parking on the left at the intersection of East
Wheelock and Grasse Road.

Note: The Velvet Rocks area is also accessible from the athletic fields near
the Hanover Co-op Food Store at 45 South Park Street. Parking near that
area, however, is limited.

6

Huntington Hill

These flowers offered a colorful sign of a human touch on an early spring day on Huntington Hill.

Vermont hills can be seen from many areas on Huntington Hill.

A range of wildlife and sweeping views of Vermont are in store for visitors to this historic farmland near the town of Lyme. A family has lived on this spot since 1794, when Andrew and Hezekiah Huntington of Norwich, CT, built a three-story house here.

Though it is private land, an easement from the New Hampshire Fish and Game Department ensures the hundreds of acres will stay undeveloped and open to the public.

Like much of the forest throughout northern New England, the trees on Huntington Hill are occasionally logged, both to generate income for the landowners and to benefit wildlife. Past caretakers of the land have received the state's Wildlife Stewards Award. Indeed, Huntington Hill's landscape of fields, hardwoods, wetlands, and ponds provides habitat for just about every mammal that lives in New Hampshire, including white-tailed deer, black bear, the occasional moose, fisher, coyote, red and gray fox, raccoon, opossum, mink, and long-tailed weasel.

Gamebirds, including wild turkey, ruffed grouse, and woodcock, also make their home here, as do raptors such as red-tailed hawks and kestrels.

The trails are especially popular with snowshoers in the winter.

SUGGESTED WALK

Huntington Hill Loop

DISTANCE: 1.13 MILES

Begin at the wildlife viewing sign at the entrance. Walk .12 miles and arrive at a clearing about 60 yards wide. Take the path on your right, near the dead stump, so the stonewall is on your right. (Don't take the path immediately to your right, which heads back to the field.)

Continue straight down this path (don't bear left) and at .22 miles, arrive at an intersection with a small white arrow sign. The farm and fields will be on your right. At .36 miles, after passing the farm, find a path on your right that leads out onto the field and enjoy the views. Continue walking and follow the path as it bends left into the hardwoods. A different field will be on your right (don't take the trail on your right to the field). At the intersection at .59 miles, bear left. At .67 miles, arrive at a four-trail intersection and take a left, toward a large standing dead tree. At .78 miles, go straight (not right). At the intersection with a lot of underbrush at .86 miles, take a right. Arrive back at the white arrow at .93 miles, and take a right to the clearing. Take a left in the clearing to return to your vehicle.

A Hooded Merganser flies over a Huntington Hill pond.

Many deciduous trees, including this red oak, thrive on Huntington Hill.

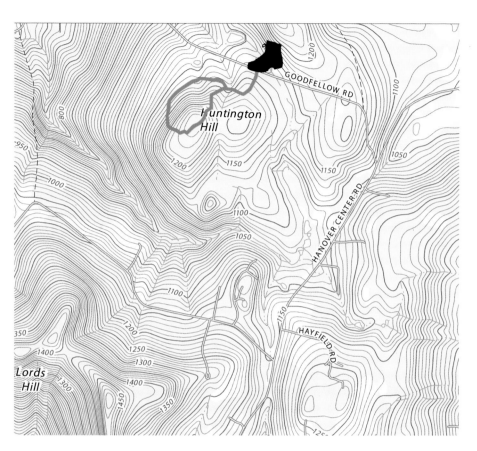

 HUNTINGTON HILL AREA INFORMATION

43º 44' 50" N

72º 11' 31" W

Total acres: 492

Miles from Hanover Inn: 6.7

Driving directions/parking: Drive north on Route 10 and take a right onto Goodfellow Road at 5.7 miles. Drive up the steep hill until the road turns to dirt at 6.5 miles, and the parking area is on the right, just before the speed limit sign, at 6.7 miles. There are four different signs that mark the entrance.

Note: Parking and paths leading onto Huntington Hill trails are also available off of Hanover Center Road northbound, on the left, about .5 miles past the northernmost intersection with Dogford Road.

7

Oak Hill

Hanover's Garipay Fields can be seen from this viewpoint on Oak Hill.

Used as cross-country ski trails in the winter, the paths on Oak Hill are spacious.

For many people, Oak Hill is synonymous with cross-country skiing, as an extensive network of trails is groomed every winter to serve as the course for Dartmouth's Division I NCAA ski team. From the 1930s to the 1950s, the hill had a rope tow and served as the primary location for downhill skiing for residents and Dartmouth students. But there are hundreds of acres to explore on Oak Hill year round, and the winding trails lead into deep woods. Indeed, though it's just two miles from downtown, it's easy to explore for hours and see no roads, buildings, or people. In April, the hill's vernal pools fill with Eastern newts and other amphibians, and in the late summer, blackberries can be found along the sunny sections of the trail. Sugar maples are tapped on the west side of the hill in early spring.

A red squirrel chatters at passersby.

SUGGESTED HIKE

Oak Hill Loop

DISTANCE: 1.42 MILES

Experience the natural environment of Oak Hill on this winding trail on the hill's summit.

Start track at signpost near the bridge. Walk .07 miles up the hill and take a right at intersection. At .20 miles, merge with another path and continue walking straight as the path turns left up the hill. There's a slight view of Fletcher Reservoir at .35 miles, and a vernal pool to the left at .40 miles. Arrive at the first numbered intersection, #29, at .53 miles. Take a hairpin left. Almost immediately arrive at intersection #18 at .55 miles and take a right. Pass a small ropes course structure at .66 miles on the left. Continue walking and see the ropes course (use by permission only) on the right at .71 miles. Continue to intersection #19 and bear left, down the hill. Soon after, at .81 miles, find a clearing to your right—a good picnic spot with views. Continue down the hill and find a bench with more views at .88 miles. At the bench take a sharp left and then take a right at 1.01 miles at #16. Then almost immediately, at #33 at 1.04 miles, take a sharp left, then take a right at #31 at 1.25 miles. Take a left when the path ends at 1.30 and, finally, take a right on trail at 1.31 miles to return to your vehicle.

Eastern Newts are plentiful in the vernal pools.

This bench offers a welcome spot to rest along a steep section of the Oak Hill trails.

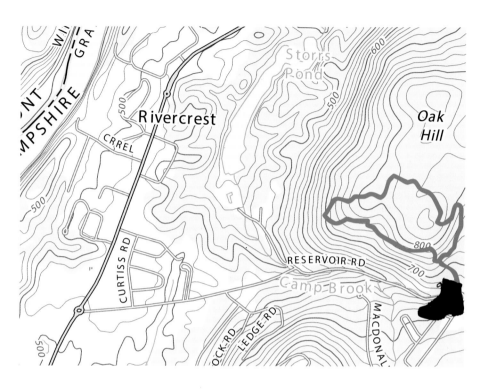

 OAK HILL AREA INFORMATION
43º 43' 09" N
72º 15' 02" W
Total acres: 493
Miles from Hanover Inn: 2.3
Driving directions/parking: Drive east on East Wheelock Street and take a left onto Grasse Road at 1.6 miles. Drive .7 miles and arrive in the grassy parking area on the right, beneath Fletcher Reservoir and just before the road sharply curves to the left, just in front of the Reservoir Road street sign. The trail head is just past the parking area, on the right.

Note: Skiing and snowshoeing on the groomed trails requires a pass, available at the Oak Hill Touring Center just off the parking lot or at the Occom Pond Ski and Skate Center. Winter walking on groomed ski trails is not allowed.

8

Mink Brook

Flowers line the first section of the Mink Brook trail.

Mink Brook's 112 acres are located about .5 miles from downtown Hanover.

Located just steps from downtown Hanover, this 112-acre preserve overseen by the Hanover Conservancy is one of the more fascinating properties in town. It is significant to the Abenaki, and the Native American tribe is still consulted when there are any major changes to the property. The land was part of the original "governor's right"—parcels that colonial governors saved for themselves when they granted new townships. In the late 1700s, state officials gave the land—an excellent source of drinking water—to Eleazar Wheelock to entice him to found Dartmouth in Hanover.

In some ways, the land is unchanged from the time that the Abenaki fished its streams and hunted its lands. In 2011, the New Hampshire Department of Fish and Game determined that a population of native brook trout—which live only in the purest waters—were flourishing in a tributary called Trout Brook. Black bear and a variety of songbirds also can be found here.

A handmade bridge connects the Quinn and Wheelock Trails.

31

SUGGESTED HIKE

Mink Brook to Trout Brook

DISTANCE: .98 MILES

The trails on the Mink Brook land are situated sort of like the Boston subway—without a surrounding loop—but they are easy to navigate.

Begin at the gate and walk straight down the path. Pass the brook on your right, arrive at an apple tree at .16 miles, and bear left. At .24 miles, leave the grassy trail and take a right, entering the woods. At .27 miles, arrive at the bridge and cross to the south side. Take a right toward Route 10 and follow blue markers. At .34 miles, take a left on the Indian Ridge Trail with orange markers. Arrive at an unmarked glade where the ferns catch the filtered sunlight and

the waters of Trout Brook tumble over moss-covered rocks at .49 miles. This is a good picnic spot. Return to Mink Brook. If you choose, take a right at the bridge and walk about .3 miles to a nice pool for wading.

Many songbirds, including this wren, can be seen and heard in Mink Brook.

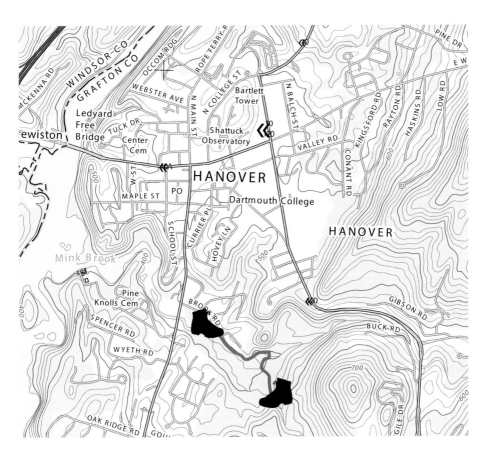

MINK BROOK AREA INFORMATION

43° 41' 31" N
72° 17' 12" W

Total acres: 112

Miles from Hanover Inn: .8

Driving directions/parking: Drive south on South Main Street for
.5 miles and take a left onto Brook Drive. Drive .3 miles and park on
right, before the gate leading into the property.

9

Moose Mountain

This bridge leads hikers over the well-maintained trail that climbs to the summit of Moose Mountain.

The summit is partially cleared and offers views to the southeast.

Moose Mountain's south peak, at 2,222 feet, is second only to the nearby north peak for the highest point in Hanover. The hike to the summit, which takes place entirely on the Appalachian Trail, offers views to the east of Cardigan Mountain. Considering the prevalence of pine trees in Hanover, the dominance of deciduous trees on the mountain is unusual. Among them are yellow birch, red and sugar maple, paper birch, moose maple, and red oak. As a result, it's a great spot for viewing the foliage in the fall. In the late summer, warblers can be spotted on the summit.

The ascent and descent of Moose Mountain is a great primer for those considering some of the more challenging hikes in the White Mountains. Visitors to New Hampshire soon learn that hiking is an integral part of the culture of the state. Some serious hikers—from teenagers to senior citizens—set out to "bag" certain mountains in New Hampshire, such as the 13 peaks in the Presidential Range or the 48 with peaks 4,000 feet or higher.

These Pink Lady's Slippers were thriving in the deep woods habitat of Moose Mountain.

SUGGESTED HIKE

Moose Mountain South Summit

DISTANCE: 3.53 MILES

This is a pleasant, direct hike through Moose Mountain's deciduous forest to the South Summit, the second highest point in Hanover. (While Moose Mountain's North Summit is slightly higher, the view from the South Summit is better.)

Begin at the trail marker opposite the parking area. Hike up the hill and reach the bridge over the stream at .22 miles. At .41 miles, reach the intersection with the Harris Trail and the Clark Pond Loop and continue straight. Cross a muddy stream at .54 miles, and continue straight, following the Appalachian Trail's white blazes, until reaching the summit at about 1.75 miles. Return the same way.

A variety of warblers, including this one, can be spotted on the summit of Moose Mountain.

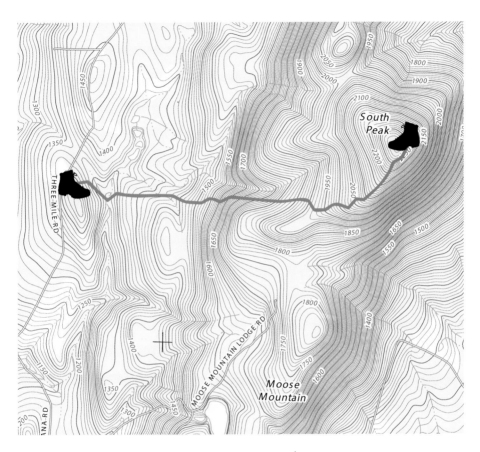

 MOOSE MOUNTAIN AREA INFORMATION

43° 43' 05" N

72° 10' 33" W

Approximate total acres: 7,436

Miles from Hanover Inn: 7.7

Driving directions/parking: Drive east on East Wheelock 4.2 miles and take a left onto Hanover Center Road. Go through "Metropolitan Downtown Etna" and, at 4.9 miles, take a right onto Ruddsboro Road. At 6.4 miles, take a left onto Three Mile Road. At 7.7 miles, see the parking area on your left.

Slade Brook

The water of Slade Brook
splashes over rocks.

This flower was found next to the parking area of Slade Brook.

The gurgling sounds of Slade Brook accompany you along the walk on this spacious trail through woods in the Jim and Evalyn Horning Natural Area at Lower Slade Brook. With a steep embankment covered with hemlocks on the north side, the meandering trail follows Slade Brook and leads to a spot from which to view a rushing waterfall. In the spring, woodland flowers dot the banks of the brook, and in the late summer and fall, a variety of mushrooms can be found poking through the leaves.

Hanover's River Road, which offers access to Slade Brook, is one of the area's more popular roads for biking. A common biking loop is to journey north on River Road to the Thetford Bridge, then to cross over into Vermont and follow Route 5 south back to the Ledyard Bridge in Norwich.

This porcupine was seen in the spring in Slade Brook.

Slade Brook Waterfall

DISTANCE: 0.8 MILES

This short trail offers a quick way to admire a pretty woodland waterfall. Begin walking at the trailhead and follow Slade Brook on your right to arrive at the waterfall at .39 miles. Return the same way. (Continuing straight will take you to Route 10.)

Following your walk, consider driving or biking farther north down River Road, one of the more scenic roads in the Upper Valley.

The waterfall can be easily viewed from the trail.

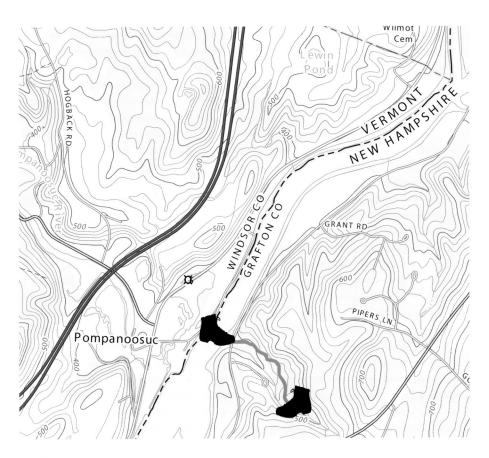

 SLADE BROOK AREA INFORMATION
43º 45' 22" N
72º 13' 23" W
Total acres: 38
Miles from Hanover Inn: 4.8
Driving directions/parking: Drive north on Route 10 and take a
left, at 4.2 miles, onto River Road. Drive for .6 miles and turn right
into a small parking area tucked off the side of the road.

FEEDBACK

We welcome thoughts about the book and the places featured. The author has worked diligently to ensure the information is accurate and helpful. Please email toptennaturalplaces@gmail.com to offer comments, corrections, and suggestions.

PEOPLE BEHIND THE BOOK

Steve Smith wrote the book and took the photos. A graduate of St. Lawrence University, he has lived with his family in Hanover since 2006.

Jermaine Johnson designed the book and served as art director. A one-time resident of Lebanon, New Hampshire, he now lives with his family in Williamsburg, Virginia.

Courtney Cania produced the maps, selected the photos, and formatted the book. A native Vermonter, Cania lives in Bradford with her husband.

Special thanks to: Richard Clark, Eli Burakian, Gail McPeek, Adair Mulligan

Dedicated to Ian and Lily